The Christmas Star

Readings And Pageants For Christmas

Frank Ramirez

CSS Publishing Company, Inc., Lima, Ohio

THE CHRISTMAS STAR:
READINGS AND PAGEANTS FOR CHRISTMAS

For more information about CSS Publishing Company resources, visit our website at
www.csspub.com or e-mail us at custserv@csspub.com or call (800) 241-4056.

ISBN 0-7880-1915-5   PRINTED IN U.S.A.

*To Doris Forney
and to the memory of Bill Forney,
for innumerable kindnesses
and most of all their constant
Christian example*

Table Of Contents

Christmas Plays

Christmas Reading And Bulletin Inserts

The Gifts Of Christmas

Characters:
  3 Teenagers
  Grandmother
  Mary
  Joseph
  Angel Gabriel
  Shepherds
  Angels
  Three Kings
  Child carrying sun
  Child carrying moon

(The backdrop consists of a giant gift box, which can be achieved by putting wrapping paper over a door near the sanctuary, as well as a giant book, consisting of two square frames, roughly the size of quilting frames with paper stretched across them. On the paper may be painted the nativity scene, and the words, "The Gifts of Christmas."
The manger with straw is in the chancel in a prominent place.
Grandma sits in a prominent place, on a rocking chair, a quilt on her lap, a book in her hands, sleeping.
In walk Three Teens. One shushes the others as they tiptoe past her. The second teen is carrying a stack of catalogs. The third has a tablet of paper and a pencil.)

One: Well, she's sleeping. That's good. Maybe we can finally figure out what we're going to get Grandmother for Christmas.

Two: It ought to be easy with these catalogs. There's bound to be a gift for her in one of these.

Three: I don't know. It seems like Grandmother's got one of everything. At least one of everything she wants.

One: Maybe. But Christmas is just around the corner, and I can't imagine not getting her a present.

Two: But think of last year. Did she really ever use those cross-country skis we got her?

Three: Or how about those skydiving lessons we got her the year before? I don't think she's redeemed them yet.

One: *(Takes a catalog)* Well, let's see. Here's Martha Stewart's catalog. Let's get her a new recipe book!

Two: That'd be great. We love her cooking.

Three: Yeah, but no one can cook like Grandma. Not even Martha Stewart. Why spoil something already perfect?

One: Maybe. Well, then, what can we get her?

Two: Here's an L. L. Bean catalog. How about getting her some new clothes? Here's a pretty nice outfit.

Three: Yeah! That's a great gift.

One: For us, you mean. These don't look like her style. What else you got?

Two: Yeah, what else do we got?

Three: Now wait, here's a good catalog. It's full of great software.

One: That might work. Grandmother loves her computer.

Two: Yeah, but she uses it to e-mail us. She really doesn't enjoy surfing the web.

Three: So what do we do?

One: I've got it. Let's ask her!

Two: Ask her to pick her own present? What's the fun of that?

One: Not while she's awake, silly.

Two: That doesn't make any sense.

Three: I think I get it! You mean we'll ask her questions real soft and she'll answer in her sleep, and then we'll really know if she needs a new robe, a new radio, or a new radiator.

(The three sneak closer to Grandmother. One puts a hand to mouth and whispers, while Two and Three cup their ears to hear what Grandmother has to say)

One: The snow has stopped falling.
Thank heavens you're sleeping.
It's time to stop stalling.
It's time to start creeping.
Dear Grandmother, resting,
Please, won't you, please tell us
Without some great testing
What someone can sell us?

Two: We'd like to buy presents
That have a great meaning.

Three: Like brandy-stuffed pheasants
And mistletoe leaning.

(Grandmother suddenly starts, her eyes closed, and stretches, while the three teens fall backwards. She then settles back down, still asleep, and begins to speak)

Grandmother: Oh, why won't they listen?
I don't need a gift.

One: But reindeer hooves glisten.
They're ready to lift
From the North Pole with Santa,
At least that's the tale.
And like them we wanta
Buy something on sale.

Grandmother: Oh, how I wish
As I sit here and slumber
My grandkids would swish
And get off of their lumber
To buy the one treasure
That comes without worry
And brings endless pleasure —
The whole Christmas Story!

(Grandmother begins to snore loudly, stretches, and then slumps a bit)

One: The whole Christmas story?

Two: The straight Christmas tale!

Three: I'm really quite sorry.
It isn't for sale.

One: Of course it isn't! We can't buy Christmas. But we can make it!

Two: Hey, you forgot to rhyme.

One: So did you!

Three: *(Takes the tablet and pencil in hand and begins to draw an angel that is displayed at the end of the speech)*
That really won't matter
If each of us seizes
The moment to scatter
And build us some pieces.

One: Pieces of what?

Two: Nativity pieces! Let's give Grandmother Christmas.

Three: Exactly! We'll make each piece out of wood or papier-mâché or soap or toothpicks! We'll put them all together and tell the Christmas story.

(The three exit hurriedly. Grandmother opens her eyes, looks to the congregation and gives them a big wink. One child runs across the stage with a sun and another with a moon, to signify a day passing. The Three Teens return)

One: Merry Christmas, Grandmother!

Two: Thank you for the nice gifts you got us.

Three: We brought you gifts too!

Grandmother: Oh, please, I don't need any presents. I have everything I want.

One: That's why we decided to give you Christmas! You put Christmas on the shelf for a month every year and then put it away in the closet.

Grandmother: Christmas! How can you give me Christmas?

Three: Just watch!

(The gift box/door opens. Out comes the child dressed as Mary, carrying a young baby)

Mary: My name is Mary, the mother of Jesus.
Our God is great and does as he pleases.
Here is this baby, born at the Census
Who sleeps in the manger that some donkey lends us!

He is the hope of the ages. For now
He is content to sleep near a cow.
Never forget he is also Messiah
Who promises always to bide his time nigh us.

Choir and/or Congregation (and Three Teens) **sing:**
Away in a manger, no crib for a bed,
The little Lord Jesus lay down his sweet head.
The stars in the bright sky look down where he lay.
The Little Lord Jesus asleep on the hay.

(Mary takes her place by the manger. The gift box opens and out comes the child dressed as Joseph)

Joseph: My name is Joseph. God has let me know
That miracles still happen here below
The heavens, and though I still feel surprise
The hope of ages here quietly lies.

Though we have had our troubles on the way
I'm happy now because upon this day
The Lord of Lords is born and I was here
To hold him and to wipe away a tear.

Choir and/or Congregation (and Three Teens) **sing:**
Oh, little town of Bethlehem, how still we see thee lie.
Above thy deep and dreamless sleep the silent stars go by.

But in thy dark streets shineth the everlasting light.
The hopes and fears of all the years are met in thee tonight.

(Joseph takes his place beside Mary. Out comes the child dressed as the Angel Gabriel)

Gabriel: I am the angel known as Gabriel
Who watched the forty days of rainfall fall.
I saw the great fish swallow Jonah and confess
That when the Red Sea parted, happiness

Fed all God's people in the desert's test.
I've stood in glory's presence but the best
Of all that I have done and seen and heard
Was telling Mary she would bear the Word.

Choir and/or Congregation (and Three Teens) **sing:**
Let all mortal flesh keep silence
And in fear and trembling stand.
Ponder nothing earthly minded
For with Blessing in his hand
Christ our God to earth descendeth,
Our full homage to demand.

One: This glorious news the angels gladly sing

Two: To shepherds to whom happy news would ring.

Three: And many shepherds heard the news we hear
Then hurried to the stable with a cheer!

Choir and/or Congregation (with Three Teens and Gabriel) **sing:**
(Shepherds enter)
Angels we have heard on high
Singing sweetly over the plains
And the mountains in reply
Echoing their glad refrain.

Gloria in excelsis deo.
Gloria in excelsis deo.

Shepherds: We love our sheep and leave them with regret
But we have seen the angels and will bet
That God will keep our sheep all safe and sound
For all the time that we are not around.

Right now we are content to seek the Lord
Who, if we fully understand the word
Of angels, has been born to us this night.
How honored are we to behold the sight.

(More Angels enter. One holds a giant star)

Angels: Then follow faithfully this happy star!
And that will show where babe and mother are!

Choir and/or Congregation (with Three Teens and Gabriel) **sing:**
It came upon a midnight clear, that glorious song of old,
From angels bending near the earth to touch their harps of gold:
"Peace on the earth, good will to all from heaven's gracious king."
The world in solemn stillness lay, to hear the angels sing.

(Suddenly all stop and put their hands to shade their eyes and look far away. Then out of the box come the Three Kings)

Choir and/or Congregation (with Three Teens, Gabriel, and Kings) **sing:**
We three kings of Orient are.
Bearing gifts we traverse afar.
Fields and fountain, moor and mountain
Following yonder star.
Star of wonder, star of light
Star of ancient beauty bright
Westward leading, still proceeding,
Guide us to thy perfect sight.

14

First King: In this chest my gold I bring.
Here's my gift, to give a king.
Out of legend, out of story,
He is greatest of all glory.

Second King: Don't be frightened. In this box
I have frankincense in stock.
How delightful is this smell.
And this king I do foretell.

Third King: It is cold. Yet I prefer
Shivering to this myrrh.
Its deep scent reminds us all
That this king someday must fall
Only to arise again
So to save us all from sin.

(The Kings take their place in the tableau)

Grandmother: How delightful. A surprise
Rarely seen by ancient eyes.
Now my Christmas is complete
With these presents at my feet.

One: Something's missing. Hear my prayer.
We must add still one more player
In this setting to make it true,
And that character is you!

Two: We are certain Jesus had
A grandma as he had a dad.
Someone who would spell his mother
Every time he'd fuss and bother!

Three: *(Leads Grandmother from her chair to the tableau. She is handed the baby Jesus)* Every one of us enjoys
Christmas time with all its toys.

Even more we must suppose
That in this story we repose.
Every one of us, it's true,
Sees baby Jesus, happy, new,
And in his mother's arms, and ours,
And charms him through the long night's hours.

One: And that's our present which we give
To all who listen, all who live.

Two: A Merry Christmas, all and one.
And now our pageant here is done.

(Close with congregational singing of "O Come, All Ye Faithful")

The End

The "Did Someone Forget To Plan" The Christmas Pageant!

There's a lot to be said for the old-fashioned Christmas pageant, in which young people rehearse diligently for a special service or performance, while elaborate sets are constructed and historically accurate costumes are sewn to fit.

On the other hand, that's a lot of work for a photo opportunity! Especially if your church is not blessed with an army of willing martyrs.

That's why I've developed what I call *The "Did Someone Forget To Plan" The Christmas Pageant!* Its purpose is simple: Tell the Christmas story for and with the children with the least amount of fuss and the greatest number of oohs and aahs possible.

Here's how it works. Collect some colorful bathrobes and swaths of cloth. Three crowns can be fashioned with cardboard, tape, and foil. Old canes become shepherd's crooks. Unsightly boxes can be transformed with some paint, foil, glue, and uncooked macaroni to become gift boxes for the magi.

Costuming is arranged the morning of the pageant during the hour prior to worship. (For some churches this is also the Sunday school hour, but we always managed to costume the play fairly quickly, so the teachers could get on with their lessons.)

The only needed set piece should be the manger. Someone can be drafted weeks in advance to make this, if you don't happen to have one from a previous year hanging around the church. Fill it with soft straw and put a blanket on top. If there's no manger available, then have Mary and Joseph stand holding the infant. In this style of pageant, we don't get hung up on details.

If there's a group of young people in your church who enjoy art projects, draft them a few weeks in advance to construct some cardboard animals for the backdrop.

As the young people arrive, cast them in the pageant. Select a different Mary every year. Wrap her in blue cloth pinned over her Sunday clothes. Select a Joseph. Brown colors work for him. Shepherds get a rougher, burlap potato sack look. Kings get the nicest looking bathrobes or swaths of cloth. They also get crowns and gifts. The youngest children make good angels, and if you have a set of white robes, you're all set.

Select three or four older youth (I usually pick junior high or high school youth) to be readers. Hand them their readings. (See below.)

Check in with the Sunday school teachers. What songs have they been learning? Those are the songs they will sing at the end of the pageant. If they haven't been learning any songs, then the congregation will become the chorus at the end of the pageant.

Check in with the accompanist. Ask that person what song would make a good backdrop for the entrance of characters. Agree with the accompanist.

Finally, consider who will play baby Jesus. I've always used the baby in our congregation born closest to the pageant with the most cooperative parents. If someone's a little leery about the process, then let them off the hook. Decide if Mary or Joseph is up to holding the baby. If not, then have Mom or Dad stand up there with the characters, in or out of costume. Remember, people love seeing a live baby Jesus.

Be an equal opportunity director. Cast baby Jesus, the kings, the shepherds, and the angels with no thought to gender or race. Mary and Joseph should probably be female and male, respectively, although I remember one year we couldn't get a boy to volunteer for that part no way, no how. In the end, one of the preteen girls dressed up as Joseph to see if she could fool her parents or not.

Introduce the pageant by saying that your church is going to tell the Christmas story in a simple way. Never make a verbal comparison during the introduction with how easy it was for everyone this year with what a headache things were last year, whether or not last year's director is still sitting in the sanctuary.

(The Accompanist begins to play a Christmas carol softly.

Mary and Joseph enter and take their places at the front of the church. Mary has a baby in her arms.

The first youth reads the following scripture text into a microphone.)

First Reader: In those days a decree went out from Emperor Augustus that all the world should be registered. This was the first registration and was taken while Quirinius was governor of Syria. All went to their own towns to be registered. Joseph also went from the town of Nazareth in Galilee to Judea, to the city of David called Bethlehem, because he was descended from the house and family of David. He went to be registered with Mary, to whom he was engaged and who was expecting a child.

Second Reader: While they were there, the time came for her to deliver her child. And she gave birth to her firstborn son and wrapped him in bands of cloth, and laid him in a manger, because there was no place for them in the inn. (Luke 2:1-7)

(Shepherds enter)

Third Reader: In that region there were shepherds living in the fields, keeping watch over their flock by night.

(Let the shepherds walk all the way to the front of the chancel, taking their place before the next reading and entrance)

(Angels enter)

Then an angel of the Lord stood before them, and the glory of the Lord shone around them, and they were terrified. But the angel said to them, "Do not be afraid; for see — I am bringing you good news of great joy for all the people: to you is born this day in the city of David a Savior, who is the Messiah, the Lord. This will be a sign for you: you will find a child wrapped in bands of cloth and lying in a manger."

First Reader: And suddenly there was with the angel a multitude of the heavenly host, praising God and saying, "Glory to God in the highest heaven, and on earth peace among those whom he favors!"

Second Reader: When the angels had left them and gone into heaven, the shepherds said to one another, "Let us go now to Bethlehem and see this thing that has taken place, which the Lord has made known to us." So they went with haste and found Mary and Joseph, and the child lying in the manger. When they saw this, they made known what had been told them about this child; and all who heard it were amazed at what the shepherds told them.

Third Reader: But Mary treasured all these words and pondered them in her heart. The shepherds returned, glorifying and praising God for all they had heard and seen, as it had been told them. (Luke 2:8-20)

(Three Kings enter)

First Reader: In the time of King Herod, after Jesus was born in Bethlehem of Judea, wise men from the East came to Jerusalem, asking, "Where is the child who has been born king of the Jews? For we observed his star at its rising, and have come to pay him homage."

Second Reader: When King Herod heard this, he was frightened, and all Jerusalem with him; and calling together all the chief priests and scribes of the people, he inquired of them where the Messiah was to be born. They told him, "In Bethlehem of Judea; for so it has been written by the prophet: 'And you, Bethlehem, in the land of Judah, are by no means least among the rulers of Judah; for from you shall come a ruler who is to shepherd my people Israel.' "

Third Reader: Then Herod secretly called for the wise men and learned from them the exact time when the star had appeared. Then he sent them to Bethlehem, saying, "Go and search diligently for the child; and when you have found him, bring me word so that I may also go and pay him homage." When they had heard the king, they set out; and there, ahead of them, went the star that they had seen at its rising, until it stopped over the place where the child was.

First Reader: When they saw that the star had stopped, they were overwhelmed with joy. On entering the house, they saw the child with Mary his mother; and they knelt down and paid him homage. Then, opening their treasure chests, they offered him gifts of gold, frankincense, and myrrh. And having been warned in a dream not to return to Herod, they left for their own country by another road.

(At this point the young people sing those songs that they may have practiced. If they have practiced no songs during Advent, then the congregation should be invited to sing a stanza or two of some favorite Christmas numbers. All the young people may then file out to accompaniment, and after removal of costumes they may return to sit with their families)

The End

The Fourth Wise Man

Director's Note: The number of the wise men has always intrigued me from the first time I read Matthew from beginning to end as a teenager and noticed that the Bible referred to magi in the plural, but didn't specify the number who set out to see the newborn king. That there were three is a familiar tradition, but there might have been two or two hundred and two, for all we know.

One day I began to wonder what a fourth wise man might have been like, and why or why not he might have set out. This play was the result.

This church play may be a little out of the ordinary for some churches, but I have produced it for small church settings. Basically the focus is on the language. I had the actors hold their books in their hands, not quite but almost Readers' Theater style. We used the Three Kings costumes which were normally used for the Christmas Pageant, and bathrobed the other actors. Although a little out of the ordinary, the play is a lot of fun.

Characters:
> Magus
> Grave Digger
> Caspar
> Melchior
> Balthazzar

Magus: The staid incantations of the djinn
Who hover 'tween the heaven and the earth
Have lost their potency. Now attend me
Powers, Principalities, for ages
The Psalters of dead Sumer have sufficed
To separate the waters from the void

22

And check Leviathan in bitter famine
Until the day of her release is come.

Till now. A star unknown invades the firmament
And ravenously burns, its bitter flame
Has blotted out the night and rivaled still
The chariot of Helios by Day.

These portents are debated by the wise
While simple souls are staring, fear the worst.

What messenger is this that dare disturb
The Universe itself and all contained
Within the sheltered walls of seven days
That sunder us from salt and thrashing sea
And utter darkness of the primal chaos?

Outside the caravan is calling all
Who seek the answers to these mysteries.
Caspar, Melchior, Balthazzar are they
Who cordon camels, leave the Persian sands
For glimpses of the sea the Roman gods
Have made their playground. Could it be the King
Foretold of old has come to us at last?

Grave Digger: Haloo! Is the Wise Man here?

Magus: Who comes now? It is the grave digger. What sort of world is it?

Grave Digger: It is a grave world, sir, a grave world.

Magus: How so?

Grave Digger: A grave and a merry thing has happened in the world today. My work is undone. The star shines in the sky, night and day, rivaling the sun in her glory, and it seems that time runs backward. Those once safely in their graves walk the street. The old are young, the dead alive, the infirm are healthy. So I come to bring you a message.

Magus: Are you messenger as well?

Grave Digger: Even so. For perhaps my services are no longer needed in this new world. And here is my message. Your brother Magi come, to seek your blessing before they leave, to beg of you what guidance you may give.

Magus: Let them approach.

(The Three Wise Men enter)

Magus: Brother Magi, what do you seek?

Caspar: We seek to know the way.

Magus: Follow the star.

Melchior: And to know whom we seek.

Magus: Perhaps it is the king, the king of the new age.

Balthazzar: And where he will be found.

Magus: The star shines bright in the Lion of Judah. Let us look into the book of Judah and see what guidance it gives. "But thou, Bethlehem, Ephrathah, though thou be little among the thousands of Judea, yet out of thee shall he come forth unto me that is to be ruler in Israel, whose goings forth have been from of old, from everlasting."

And so it might be said that a little child shall lead them. Bethlehem. The House of Bread. Perhaps the Bread of Life shall issue forth from your city's gates.

And now my own question to you. If you go forth to see the king, what gifts do you bring? Caspar?

Caspar: Born a king on Bethlehem's plain
Gold I bring to crown him again
King for ever, ceasing never,
Over us all to reign.

Magus: How much of our strife is caused by gold? How wise it is to empty our coffers into the hold of the king. And you, Melchior?

Melchior: Frankincense to offer have I
Incense owns a deity nigh.
Prayer and praising All men raising
Worship him God on high.

Magus: Ah, the fragrance of frankincense is conducive to thought. How easily thought is perverted to contemplate the evil use of God's gifts. Let the peace of the scent remind us all that God's gift of mind must be used wisely. And you, Balthazzar. What do you carry in your packs?

Balthazzar: Myrrh is mine. Its bitter perfume
Breathes a life of gathering gloom
Sorrowing, sighing, bleeding, dying,
sealed in the stone cold tomb.

Magus: Your words are hard, and their meaning is for the time hidden. The tomb waits for all, until death is conquered.

Three Kings: *(Together)* We three kings of Orient are
Bearing Gifts we traverse afar.
Field and fountain, moor and mountain,
Following Yonder Star.
O Star of Wonder, star of night
Star with royal beauty bright.
Westward leading, still proceeding,
Guide us to thy perfect light.

Magus: Let us travel together, for behold, the new age is coming, an age of reconciliation, an age when the light shall shine for the nations. Time is turning backwards. Let us seek out this new king, a king not of might or power in arms, but a king of love.

The End

The Ten Commandments Of Christmas

Seasons don't begin and end in a single day. There is no mad rush in autumn to do all the leaf raking and storm windowing in an hour. We don't brace for a single day of winter or hurriedly plant during a frenzied day of spring, or cram three months' worth of living into a solitary day of summer.

If a summer picnic is rained out, we know we can plan for another weekend. The first leaves of autumn are only the beginning. One snowflake does not a winter make.

Seasons don't come and go in a day, but that's the way we treat Christmas. For most of us the holiday begins around sunset on Christmas Eve. Christmas is usually composed of one part worship service, three parts last second shopping and wrapping, two parts frantic driving between one relative and another, and five parts total collapse.

The following day we put away the Christmas albums we never got around to enjoying, dump the tree in the burnpile, and sullenly wonder what happened to the holiday, while brooding over the ominous arrival of the New Year.

Not a pretty sight, is it?

The church calendar knows nothing of this frenetic holiday. For Christendom, Christmas is a season that begins with the first Sunday of Advent and continues through the feast of the Magi, known as Epiphany (January 6). Each week has a different focus of celebration and worship. In many countries gifts are given on December 6 or January 6 and many of the days in between. To cease singing Christmas carols on December 25 would strike Christians around the world as ludicrous.

This year you should plan for the long haul, to make Christmas a season, not a day. And that requires some serious resolutions. Here are my Ten Commandments of Christmas.

1. Honor the Lord of the season with pleasure, not through deprivation or some misplaced sense of solemnity. We have been waiting all year for the King's arrival. This is a holiday. Keep it holy by celebrating with friends and family.
2. Let your gift giving be joyful.
3. You shall not be a slave to greeting cards.
4. You shall scatter your trips through the season.
5. You shall do one thing you have never done.
6. You shall destroy one sacred cow, ignore one holiday tradition, to give yourself more time. The babe will arrive whether your special fudge is made or not.
7. You shall play with the nativity set this Christmas.
8. Be resolved that December 26 is as much Christmas as the day before. (If nothing else, this allows you to take advantage of the sales. Did you never think what great gifts you could give to people if they would only wait until December 27?) Play a Christmas album loud enough to embarrass someone. (It doesn't matter which: Perry Como, the Chipmunks, or the new Hymnal Masterworks CD.)
9. You shall visit one shut-in during the season, and invite one lonely person into your home. Hospitality is part of the season. There was no room at the inn. Too often we have a mandatory guest list of people we have to entertain or visit. Tear it up. Pick something new to do this year.
10. Sometime around December 30, when the house is quiet except for the creaking of the boards and the chimes of midnight, sing "The Little Drummer Boy," "O Little Town of Bethlehem," or "Silent Night" quietly to yourself. Welcome the King.

If

(with apologies to Rudyard Kipling)

If you can drape the tinsel clinging
On branches hewn from mountains far away
But still imagine heaven's angels singing
Through the cold of a distant Christmas day;

If you can place a star precarious
Atop it all for wondering children fine
And not forget the real star was glorious
And lured the Magi to pursue the sign;

If you can see in every woman waiting
The miracle that set the world aflame
And see past shoppers with their tempers grating
And pretend that it's the census — leave your name;

If you can wait in line for hours for nothing
And know that time is never spent for naught
For when the inns are closed and day is waning
The stable waits for those who have been caught;

If you can these imagine and one other
Amid the cares the season seems to sow,
If you can see in all a sister or a brother
And in every seed a chance to grow;

Then you may look on Mary's face and know the wonders
Of the grace that buries pain in new life's glow.
As her strength returns her gentle tune meanders.
She softly rocks the infant to and fro.

And you may kneel with the oxen by the manger
And let the fingers of the only Lord of Life
Bat the air and keep you safe from every danger
Though life's cares we balance edgewise on a knife.

Let the waves of life explode against the beaches
And crash on rocky shores to no avail
Because the world is captured when the infant stretches
Who will champion the outcast and the frail.

There is comfort for the ones who are not coping.
There is warmth for those in cold who wait for day.
For the weary and the sinners there is hoping.
There is still a Christ in Christmas if you pray.

Bethlehem's Star

'Twas the night before Christmas and Bethlehem's star
Shone brightly to call forth the kings from afar.

The shepherds were watching their sheep when the sky
Was filled with the angels who sang low and high
That Jesus had come to his people at last
To conquer the wrongs that were done in the past.

These shepherds saw angels and knew right away
That Jesus had come to proclaim the new day.

But who was this Jesus and where did he rest?
And where were the others, the better and best
Who should have been watching for signs in the night?
While frost was far sprinkled, the winter's winds bite
And comfort prevents those who waited so long
From hearing the blessings that came from the song.

"All Glory to God" was what Gabriel sang
And bouncing off hills his voice echoed and rang.

The birds cry unechoed in dim dewy groves
Like leaves in deep forests where nobody goes
That fall, uncollected, in layers for years
Untouched by the grottoes of yesterday's tears.

So too all our sorrows uncounted have been
Forgotten, unnoticed by history's pen.
Did anyone mark when we cried? Or in vain
Did hopes our Redeemer would come slowly wane?

31

No, God saw it all, for his angels record
The fall of a sparrow, the softest kind word,
And the wish for a kingdom of justice and light.
Not by accident did he a stable by night
Choose to enter the world. No mistake makes our Lord
Who chose such a moment to enter the world.

In the still quiet hours 'twixt sunset and morn
His cries told a mother a baby was born.

The time was eternal as every birth seems
But when it was over the Timeless of Dreams,
The Ancient of Days took a shape and his hands
Seemed to aimlessly wave but in all of God's lands
Whether valley or mountain, or white coastal bar.
They've heard of this babe and of Bethlehem's star.

The Christmas Star

> "For we observed his star at its rising, and have
> come to pay him homage."   — Matthew 2:2

This is the time of the year when your family probably gets out the nativity set. In addition to little statues of Mary, Joseph, Jesus, and the angels, your set probably includes sheep, donkeys, shepherds, a star that fits on the roof of the stable, and three kings. The kings are shown following the Star of Bethlehem, bearing gifts for the Christ child.

Every year at this time planetariums across the country run similar programs on the Christmas Star. The purpose of the shows is to theorize what it was that the Wise Men saw before they traveled west to find the infant Jesus. They usually point to a conjunction of Jupiter and Saturn that occurred around 8 B.C.

Many people refer to the "three kings." The Gospel of Matthew does not tell us how many "kings" there were, but the Bible is clear that they were not kings. They were Magi, or magicians. They were both astronomers and astrologers. They were astronomers because they studied the sky and astrologers because they thought they could fortell the future this way.

According to Matthew, after they arrived in Jerusalem they told Herod the Great they were looking for a king. Herod was furious that there was another king in his kingdom, but he hid his anger and made them promise to reveal this infant when they found him. The Magi indeed found Jesus, but were instructed in a dream to travel home by a different way and avoid Herod. This threw the mad king into a rage, and he decided to slaughter all boys under the age of two in order to kill Jesus.

Many believe that Herod the Great died in 4 B.C. This is based on the account of the ancient historian Josephus, who said that

Herod died between a lunar eclipse and Passover. And because Herod commanded that children two years and younger be killed upon his death, many people believe Jesus was born around the year 6 or 7 B.C.

John Mosley of Griffith Observatory thinks they are all wrong. He has a different theory which seems to fit the facts better. According to Mosley (whose ideas are found in a little book called *The Christmas Star*, published by Griffith Observatory), you have to remember that the Magi were astronomers. Their "magic" consisted of trying to read the stars in order to foretell the future. What, Mosley wondered, would attract their attention?

Some have wondered if perhaps the Star of Bethlehem was a comet or a nova (exploding star). But comets in the ancient world were thought to foretell disasters. No one would have thought a comet pointed to the prince of peace. And the Chinese, who have kept meticulous astronomical records for thousands of years, do not record any exploding stars for the period near the birth of Jesus.

But especially interesting to ancient astronomers were the wandering stars, or planets, which seem to move over the weeks against the background stars. And the most interesting thing that occurred in the skies that might have attracted the Magi was a conjunction of Jupiter and Saturn, when they appeared to draw close together in the sky.

It turns out that Jupiter, the king of heaven (in the eyes of the Magi), and Venus, the queen of heaven and brightest object in the sky after the Sun and Moon, drew very close right before sunrise on August 12 of 3 B.C. This conjunction took place in the constellation of Leo, the Lion. The Lion was associated with Judea in the ancient world, and that constellation also contains Regulus, the King Star. Almost a year later, on June 17, 2 B.C., right after sunset, the two planets seemed to touch. This also took place in the same constellation. And three times between those conjunctions Jupiter nearly touched Regulus itself on September 14 of 3 B.C. and February 17 and May 8 of 2 B.C.

To us this might mean nothing, and it certainly did not attract the attention of anyone in Herod the Great's court. They were not astronomers. But to the Magi the message was clear. A mighty

34

king was coming, and he would be born in Judea. Naturally they would travel to the capital, Jerusalem, to find out about this king, and just as naturally Herod would not know what they were talking about. The "Christmas Star" had occurred in plain sight and no one had known it!

These events seem to have happened after the death of Herod the Great in 4 B.C. But Mosley has an answer for that too. The key event that dates the mad king's death is that lunar eclipse, which is when the earth travels between the moon and sun. The moon typically turns red, and in the ancient world it was seen as bad luck.

But a total eclipse that fits the bill occurred on January 9, 1 B.C. According to the ancient historian Josephus, Herod died between this eclipse and Passover, which fell on April 8 of that year.

So Jesus would have been born before this time, probably near the occasion of the "Oath of Allegiance" to Caesar Augustus on the occasion of his Silver Jubilee, the twenty-fifth anniversary of the awarding of his title "Father of the Country." Joseph would have had to travel to Bethlehem to register around 3 or 2 B.C.

None of this means that astrology works. It tells us, however, what could have gotten the attention of the Magi when they looked into the sky.

A century later the martyr Ignatius wrote regarding this star, "Thence was destroyed all magic, and every bond vanished; evil's ignorance was abolished, the old kingdom perished, God being revealed as human to bring newness of Eternal Life."

When you look into the sky at night you can still see the Christmas star. Sort of. Check a star chart to find out when Jupiter and Venus will be visible in the heavens. And remember, every now and then they get together and seem very nearly to touch. It's quite a sight. And it's no wonder that it drew the Magi to seek the King of Kings.

Christmas In A Different Context

Read Luke 2:1-20.

There's a little piece making the rounds right now on the Internet called "The Top Ten Excuses The Innkeeper Gave Joseph And Mary." As is usual with such jokes making the rounds of e-mail, no author is listed. It includes such excuses as: "Roman's Stay Free promotion a bit too successful," "Wife said he couldn't accept wood carvings as payment anymore," and "Last pregnant lady riding a donkey took all their towels."

The list reminds us of one of our basic assumptions about the Christmas story, that there was no room anywhere for Mary and Joseph when Jesus was born.

There was no room at the inn, that was for certain. I remember the Las Posadas pageants which we studied and performed at church. Joseph and Mary went from place to place, solemnly pleading for help, but always there was no room for them at the inn.

So what was left for the holy couple but to accept the offer of a stable? Jesus was born in a barn. When I was in the sixth grade it was my turn to play Joseph at the Christmas pageant at St. Frances of Rome Church in Azusa, California. We had straw and a manger and a wrapped-up doll. No live animals. I think there were cardboard cutouts of sheep and cows. We were city kids. I'm not sure we'd have done too well around real animals.

It's not surprising there was no room at the inn. That still happens today. In Indiana when we have as insignificant an event as a Notre Dame home football game, there is no room at the inn for a fifty mile radius. A real life Roman census probably turned every burg in Judea into a convention town.

But if there was no room at the inn there was still hospitality. And in the Middle East, hospitality was more than a virtue. It was an honor, a privilege, and great fun. The idea of having unknown guests was a treat. If you had an unexpected guest, Jewish law permitted you to take an animal from your neighbor without asking permission just so you could feed the guest in style. Pay for it later. And the neighbor would understand.

When the disciples got a little nervous about 5,000 people and their families listening to Jesus close to dinner time, they suggested that all the people go to the neighboring villages. They weren't copping out. They just knew you could count on people feeding people.

I was reading the first volume of John Nolland's *Word Biblical Commentary* on Luke one autumn, looking ahead to my Christmas messages that year. Nolland is a biblical instructor from Bristol, England. In the space of a simple paragraph describing the Christmas story, he pointed out that one typical design of a Palestinian home of that era would house both the people and the animals under a single roof. The animal portion of the dwelling would be a half step down from the people part.

In other words, Joseph and Mary did what anyone else would do who could not find room in an inn. They sought and found shelter in a private home. There were probably several families potlucking it, sharing what they had together with the host family. Perhaps some were from the same village. Others might be total strangers. Either way, there'd be stories to share.

And a new baby. Babies have this marvelous way of just coming when they want to. Mary and Joseph, nervous perhaps about their first child, and maybe not recognizing at first the labor pains for what they were, would soon have quick confirmation from their new neighbors that the pressure and then the pain was the sign that a natural process was underway, and it was unlikely to go away.

The birth, a grand adventure, left everyone flushed and excited. People who are present at a birth feel half weepy and half exalted. They know they've been present at the most godlike moment a human can share. After all, even though this is the Son of God, the most significant birth of all time, the Messiah, King of Kings, Lord of Lords, Prince of Peace, this is also a baby!

And there was room for the baby. Maybe not at the inn. But in someone's home. The assumption I've lived with was wrong. There *was* room for the babe. It wasn't a barn. It was a home.

Which changes a lot, as far as I'm concerned. Because I always figured I could do better than people who pointed to the barn around back and said, you can stay there if you like, just don't make any noise and wake us up. The Holy Family was invited into someone's home and shared the incredible moment of birth with strangers and perhaps friends who were forever changed because they'd been present at the birth. Now that's a challenge.

There's a world of refugees out there, a world of babies waiting to be born, a world of people travelling from here to there. They're knocking at the door. They need a place to stay. Good homes used to be built with a guest room because you just never knew. That's not the case anymore. Most of us don't have room in our homes, much less our hearts.

Merry Christmas. The community of God came through when it had to, 2,000 years ago. Will we continue to come through? There's an empty room in my house at this time, now that my oldest has flown to college. Is there room in my heart as well?

Holy Night. Silent Night.
I'd always hoped it'd come out right.
They found room and so can we.
No one said the ride was free.
Humans and angels both sing.
Sleep, my baby, my king.